CW01187270

Enduring Polish Courage

An account of World War Two
internment, escape and freedom

By Christine Kaminska-Smith, MA

To Chrissie,
Love Christine X

Witold Lucjan Kaminski

DEDICATION

This book is dedicated to my brother, Peter and all the descendants from Lucien Kayworth (nee Witold Lucjan Kaminski). Telling his story has been both a learning process and a great pleasure to further understand my courageous father.

As with most of those who experienced times of extreme deprivation and deep fear during WW11, my father hardly spoke of his journey and his difficulties. This book is written as a mainly factual account taken from copies of original documents including his own detailed descriptions of events, often mentioning people who helped him. His debriefing document, written on landing in Britain is in his own hand and with it he speaks across the decades.

Acknowledgements

This account of what slowly evolved as the telling of a story that began in Poland and ended in Scarborough, Yorkshire has led me through paths during World War Two that I would never have envisioned. My brother had suggested I write this during Covid as our father`s testament to courage, youth and determination. His courage endured, even to his last days and I am proud of him and my Polish heritage.

Along the journey I am indebted to many people:

Jana Buresova for giving me an outline of the flight from Eastern Europe of many refugees and military personnel.

Michal Tabakowski, a Polish friend of my son-in-law

Tomasz Jachyra, another Polish friend of my son-in-law

Elzbieta Tabakowska, who translated the very important document of my father's debriefing and upon which I have based an accurate account of his journey.

The Polish (Sikorski) Institute, for two documents from the archives, ref No. LOT-AV96/21/24 and a copy of an entry from the Encyklopedia of the Polish Air Force N.C.O's Training School, 1993.

The Swiss Tracing Service for a copy of a personal document file ref E5791 1000/949, ref 1/10029 which was also translated into English.

Helpful books for background and added information:

Roger Moorhouse, *First to Fight* Vintage 2020

Lynne Olsen and Stanley Cloud, *A Question of Honor* Knopf 2003

Jan Karski, *Story of a Secret State* Penguin 2019

Adam Zamoyski, *The Forgotten Few, The Polish Air Force in the Second World War* 2009

Adam Zamoyski, *Poland – a History* Harper Collins, 1987

Robert Winder, *Bloody Foreigners, The Story of Immigration to Britain* Abacus 2013

Last and not least, my partner Barry who kept steadfast confidence in my research and my family who were excited and always wanted to know progress when the writing began.

Contents

British Library Cataloguing-in-Publication Data

A catalogue record for this book is available from the British Library

ISBN 978-1-916722-04-02

Printed by Sarsen Press Ltd, Winchester.

Introduction

I always knew my father was a 'foreigner'. He spoke with an accent and wasn't like other girls' fathers. But when I was about 9 and we were asked at school "what does your Daddy do and where is he from?" I thought I had better ask. I was told, quite forcefully I remember, that I was to say that he was French. My mother called him 'Lucien' and I had heard him speaking French so it seemed a reasonable thing to say. I wasn't to know at that point that covering up his Polish heritage and saying he was French were important in various ways in the middle of the 1950s. It seemed unimportant at the time as we all knew he was Polish. Although my brother and I were never taught Polish as children, we were to be brought up to be `British` and we had lots of Polish friends of my father`s which added to the unlikely ruse of being French.

He was a bright and bubbly Dad; always laughing and tinkering with something, whether it was a radio, stereo system or, eventually a car which lived in our front garden. He had to dig out the garden first and thereafter he always seemed to be under the car mending something.

He rarely talked about the War but I knew he had had a bad time and as a young girl I couldn't bear to hear the general reports of killing and dying and to know that he had been involved. Little was I to know then that more than 70 years later my brother was to show me a large folder with all the documents my father and mother had kept during the War and after, together with photographs and postcards he had sent back to Poland during that time. Intriguing and informative, so this quest began to find the details of his story from the outbreak of war in Poland to his arrival in England, marriage to my mother and the further difficulties that lay ahead.

He was born in Grudziadz, a medium sized town in Northern Poland in 1919 (or maybe 1920, he seemed to change the year from time to time). Grudziadz is a city of former West Prussia. After the devastating floods of the Vistula River in 1560, large sections of the area were depopulated. This territory was then taken over by Dutch settlers, mainly Mennonites who were given freedom of religion, their own schools and the transportation of their products along the Vistula free of taxes. In the 17th century Mennonites predominated in the villages of Parsken,

Kommerau, Klein-Lubin and Dragsass. In addition, they were numerous in the villages of Klein-Wolz, Tresch, Gross-Lubin and Klein-Lubin. Thus by 1900 Grudziadz was a city of strong and promising growth caused by the development of the city in general. It was called the 'city of schools', and it was centrally located for the three religious congregations at that time, Catholics, Annabaptist Mennonites and Methodists.

My grandfather worked for the Civil Service in Grudziadz. Life before the war I have to ascertain had been pretty good. They lived in a large flat and I have photographs showing the family in good clothes enjoying skating and horse riding plus they had a summer residence in the country. My father spoke very little about his family in Poland but from his immaculate table manners (which were to stand him in good stead later) and his general air of knowing what to say and do, his Eastern European heritage shone through the hardships during the War and those that were to follow throughout his life.

Following four years at grammar school, in 1936 my father was enrolled in a military unit in Poland for non-commissioned minors (Szkola pdoficerw Lotnietwa dia Maloletnich), in Bydgoszcz, Poland. He completed the shortened and modified course in Krosno in 1939, qualifying as an Aircraft Mechanic. His results were pretty average and then all training ceased because of the outbreak of war in September 1939 and he, together with the majority of the students were evacuated from Luck to Romania. With the rest of the cadets he crossed the Romanian border near Luck on the specific command of his Lieutenant colonel.

Poland and Romania had been on friendly terms since long before World War One and in 1921 Poland and Romania signed a mutual defence treaty. It wasn't expected that Romania would join the war, but they did agree to accept delivery of new fighter planes that the British and French had shipped to the Polish Air Force. Reasonably safe refuge was given to units of cadets and this must have been the last whereabouts of his son that my grandfather could find.

My father`s particular group of cadets was held in September 1939 at Slatina Olt camp, Romania which is now a holiday camp area next to the Adriatic Sea. Dad must have found captivity intolerable and escape was an imperative. He left the camp on his own aiming to reach France. He was helped by the Polish Consulate in Romania and finally crossed the Romanian border en route to France. The Poles always had the fight for the freedom of Poland on their minds. Their sense of duty, love for their country and independence drove them forward. In addition, they had received specific orders for all the armed forces to get to France and then Britain as soon as possible for the mounting war effort.

In Bucharest, General Stanislaw Ujeski, a top Polish Air Force official, set up a secret evacuation centre where Polish embassy officials forged passports and visas and invented false names for the holders. Many Poles escaped on their own (and my father was one of them) but others were helped by couriers and phoney identification papers. In various camps men slipped away and many pilots escaped in this way.

Throughout Romania, young Poles were hitching rides on trucks, finding their way through forests and fields, stowing away on trains, all the time dodging German agents and patrols. In Bucharest, pilots were given money and directed by Polish officials to safe hotels and the evacuation centre. New passport photos were taken and the Poles were packed into mainly merchant ships to continue the long sea journey to France. In all, more than 10,000 Polish Air Force pilots and ground crew, assisted by the underground networks of the government-in-exile managed to escape Poland after the German invasion, together with thousands of soldiers and sailors.

The journeys were long and arduous and lasted days, weeks or more. Some men travelled from the Baltic to Sweden and on to Denmark, Holland and Belgium. Others went from the Black Sea to the Mediterranean, Lebanon and Egypt. Some walked or skied across the Carpathian mountains or headed east from Poland to Soviet ports aboard merchant ships. This extraordinary movement of men from Poland was unmatched by any other country during WW2. In all more than 8,000 men or 75% of the Polish Air Force made it from France to Britain. However, many of the ground troops were either killed, captured or interned; only a small number, 20,000, made it across the Channel, many of those thanks to the British at Dunkirk.

My father's route to France was circuitous. From Constantinople (now Istanbul) he went on board the French ocean liner 'SS Paris' via Malta and into Marseille, eventually being incorporated into the Polish forces at Lyon-Bron in France. The 'SS Paris' was a French ocean liner completed in 1921 and was the largest liner under the French flag. It was one of the finest liners put into service at that time. He arrived in Marseille in November 1939.

Meanwhile, back home in Grudziadz with the Russians already having invaded Poland, my grandfather had lost touch with my father and asked the Red Cross for help to find the whereabouts of his son. My own research with the Red Cross has confirmed that my grandfather had enquired twice about news of his son; once in December 1939 and again in January, 1940. The Red Cross had lost touch with my father in Romania and all trace of him had stopped. The file containing the original letters from my grandfather has now been destroyed.

It is more than probable that my father never saw his father again. No doubt the Russians saw my grandfather as a threat and assumed or possibly knew that he may have worked for the Germans. He was taken outside, put against a wall and shot. The Russians went through Poland quickly. My grandmother was raped by a Russian and my aunt Maryla (probably age 14 or 15) was protected by my grandmother insisting that she was ill with chickenpox, and covered in spots.

Grandfather

Dad, Grandmother and Maryla

Grandfather and Dad

France, Internment and Escape

In April 1940 my father was assigned to Infantry Division 11. Partisan units had been organised and were kept moving south east in order to gain supplies of food and munitions and then to regroup once the Russians had entered the war on 17 September, 1939. My father was a reservist and one could ask why he joined the army and didn't escape to meld into the east or perhaps make his way to Australia (as so many did). This is to misunderstand the spirit and courage of the Poles. First and foremost, the Poles were 'individualists' and, secondly, hugely nationalistic. Their strong sense of unity in adversity meant that defeat in war entailed unique and drastic consequences. Their feelings were that when just one Polish soldier was beaten on the battlefield, total annihilation could be possible for the entire nation. The attitude of the Poles to WW11 was different; it was their own war.

Poland had been overrun with the Germans and the Russians. In addition, all men 'on the run' were told to sign up and join the army in Lyon and continue to fight to get their country back. The Polish Government-in-exile for the first year of the war operated from Paris with Lyon the centre of The French Resistance. The most important resistance networks were created there and Lyon became the centre of Polish Resistance until 1943.

The official government of the Polish Republic was re-established in Paris on 30 September 1939 in accordance with the Constitution of 1935 which gave exceptional powers to the president in the event of war. General Sikorski had flown to England the previous June for an urgent meeting with Churchill. He asked if Britain would rescue Polish forces so they could fight again. Churchill responded "Tell your army in France that we are their comrades in life and in death". He added "We shall conquer together or we will die together". Notices were broadcast by Sikorski that Poland would continue to resist and he ordered Poles in France to head immediately south to ports where Polish and British ships were ready to pick them up.

The Polish Government was set up at the Hotel Regina at the corner of the Rue de Rivoli, Paris and the Polish Air Force was established on the 2nd floor. General Sikorski was appointed Prime Minister and took over the duties of the interned Polish Government. Focusing on the Air Force, he wanted to move the whole of the Polish Air Force to Britain as the Poles had experience of British aero engines. However, Sikorski`s government-in-exile was then officially transferred to Angers in November 1939. As the seat of the Polish Government, many foreign ambassadors and ministers resided officially at Angers. Orders came from General Sikorski that all young Poles should try to escape to France. These orders applied particularly to pilots, mechanics, sailors and artillery men.

By the summer of 1940 London had become the home of the displaced governments-in-exile of five Nazi occupied countries: Poland, Czechoslovakia, Holland, Belgium and Norway. Since the start of the war more than 30,000 Polish airmen, sailors and soldiers had made their way to Britain and the Poles were the largest foreign military force in Britain; the airmen numbering 8,500.

Arriving in Marseille in November, 1939 my father was assigned to the 23 Bron reserve squadron and then transferred to the Second Division of Chasseurs. This was formed from various branches of the French Army. Established in 1743 Chasseurs or `Chasseurs a pied` were light-infantry regiments. After WW1 there were 31 battalions of Chasseurs mainly put together for administrative purposes but grouped into demibrigades of three battalions for war.

Historically and in handed down folklore, young Poles had a fascination with airplanes and flying. Previously, many of Poland's most dashing figures had come from the cavalry and in the sixteenth and seventeenth centuries mounted warriors were one of the keys to its military might. The Polish cavalry was renowned and feared, in particular the Husaria who were heavily armed and highly mobile. Their intentions were to crush enemy defences in lightning charges.

After WW1 the exploits of the Husaria faded into history and they became relics. After the country was finally freed from the subjugation of the Russians, Germans and the Austrians the younger generation of Poles turned to other heroes and they found them in flying.

My father was on the front line of the war for a short time, just a matter of weeks when he was ordered by his Polish commander and other senior figures to cross and enter the Swiss border. During his time in the light-infantry he served as an instructor in the artillery arsenal and was given the rank of corporal.

He was some way away from his Air Cadet training at this point and to put into context how popular and difficult it was to join the Cadet Corps, by 1936 more than 6,000 young men were competing for only 90 places. They came from all sections of society, landowner's sons, peasants, teachers and miners. They received instruction on how to act like a gentleman, always to bring a lady flowers and always kiss a lady's hand, on arrival and departure. An officer, gentleman and a pilot did not gamble, boast or drink to excess. "Remember", the Cadet's Code stated, "that you are a worthy successor to the Husaria and of the pioneers of Polish aviation. Remember to be chivalrous always and everywhere."

At the outbreak of WWII the Swiss had been required by the Geneva Convention of 1929 to keep soldiers from Poland and other allies interned until the end of hostilities. In 1939 Wauwilermoos internment camp held 10,082 Polish soldiers.

In 1940 there was a mass migration and huge numbers of Poles had fled independently to Switzerland. They were promptly interned and used as manual labour. In total, 12,000 soldiers were interned and not allowed to fraternise; 400 were allowed to continue their studies. My father's first internment camp was at Ursenbach, Kanton Bern from June to December, 1940. Swiss internment camps were more like prison camps. Wauwilermoos is probably the most famous. It was established in 1940 and internees included Allied soldiers, some from the United States Army Air Forces.

Conditions were described as `intolerable`. Beds were often wooden planks or sometimes just straw on the floor. Americans, in particular, were treated badly and subjected to physical and sexual abuse, starvation, freezing conditions and virtually no hygiene facilities.

It is not known if my father was treated to these conditions. As he was only 20 at the time he was probably allowed to finish his studies. He remarks in his 'debrief' on landing in England that he finished his 5th year of Air Cadet Corps studies. No doubt he was billeted with other Polish cadets. Photographs that we have from the time show him with groups of young men enjoying themselves. Smiling and joking, there was obviously camaraderie between them. However, he was sent to work and documents show that he worked for some weeks in a foundry in Ursenbach as a moulder in a machine shop. Luckily, the regulations of the time included stamping and signing important documents so we have a written reference for work which had been approved with a very readable stamp from Roche la Moliere in the Loire region and dated April, 1942. This reference had been asked for by the Swiss authorities in February 1941. Possibly the reference had been slow in signing and returning but it is evidence that he was in the Loire region during his time in Swiss internment. However, there is more to his story in internment.

From a detailed document that I obtained (as his daughter) from the Swiss authorities, there was an altercation which led to trial and punishment. He had already been transferred to Madiswil camp, Kanton Bern from 1 December 1941 until 1 March and again from 15 May to July to camp Affeltkangen. He was sent to camp Wetzikon in the area of Kanton Zurich for a short time. After only a few weeks after his next transfer to camp Gossau he was interrogated and suspected (but hadn't confessed) of assisting his fellow internee Krysczukajtis to escape. In addition, he was charged that he left his work place without permission, stayed overnight from 26 to 27 October, 1941 without a valid reason, resisted a planned transfer, resisted the instructions of a guard and, most importantly, threatened the commander of Gossau, Lt. Wildbolz. He was sent to prison in Tobel, Kanton Thurgau punishable with ten days detention. No doubt this penal prison was markedly different to the internment camps where he had been allowed to leave camp and work in the community. The evidence showed that he was held for disobedience by military court and also for threat. A preliminary investigation was made.

On 11 December 1941 investigations went ahead and on 26 February 1942 the Territorial Court considered its findings. It seems my father was not present at the proceedings. He had disappeared.

The charges included: failure to comply with rules and regulations, repeated offenses against a guard, disobedience, repeated abuse and threat. Apparently, according to the Court, he left his work place at the farm Luedi in Bertschikon by bicycle on 17 October and 18 October and went to Gossau and Ottikon to talk to his fellow soldier Kryszcukati who was in detention at the time. The records held by the Swiss stated that he left his work place twice on a bicycle in order to visit his fellow soldier. Internees were firstly not allowed to use bicycles and secondly not to leave their work place. It is interesting that he had been working at a farm in Switzerland; my mother said in later years that he had been helped to escape by a Swiss farmer and it may well have been this man.

My father could be difficult sometimes and in times of war as a young man it may be surprising that he did not obey orders. When he received an order from one of the guards to be ready at 6.40 a.m for a transfer, he decided to chat to his fellow soldiers. He was ordered by the guard again to get ready but he didn't obey, "packing and unpacking a box with his belongings several times, chatting to his fellow soldiers, and then finally told Zuercher the guard that he or camp commander Lt. Wildbolz could not order him to do anything, he, the accused would say himself if he wanted to leave or not." In Zuercher's office he refused again to pack his things and said he would do what he wanted. Following this he was slapped in the face by Zuercher. His response was "Boo, the Swiss guards". His behaviour was described as "stubborn" and apparently my father said to Lt. Wildbolz that "he could do anything to him, he would be able to do anything, he would know where to find Wildbolz to settle

Cadets, 1938

things with him." Surprising behaviour by a youngster (he would be 20 at that time) at a time of war. Whether he was emboldened by his Polish heritage and fervour for active duty is difficult to say but it must have been the deciding factor to escape and, as General Sikorski had ordered, join the escaping Poles and get to England.

The defendant was found guilty in his absence, and was sentenced to six months imprisonment and also to bear the court costs, which of course were never paid.

Some time at the end of 1941 my father disappeared. He was probably helped or hidden by the Swiss farmer but I recall him saying, when we were children, that he walked across the Alps in the winter and all he had to eat were potatoes that he had dug up. We didn't know then the significance that this small nugget in his escape story referred to but it seemed romantic and far away.

Krosno, 1939

1940

Internment 1940

Internment 1941

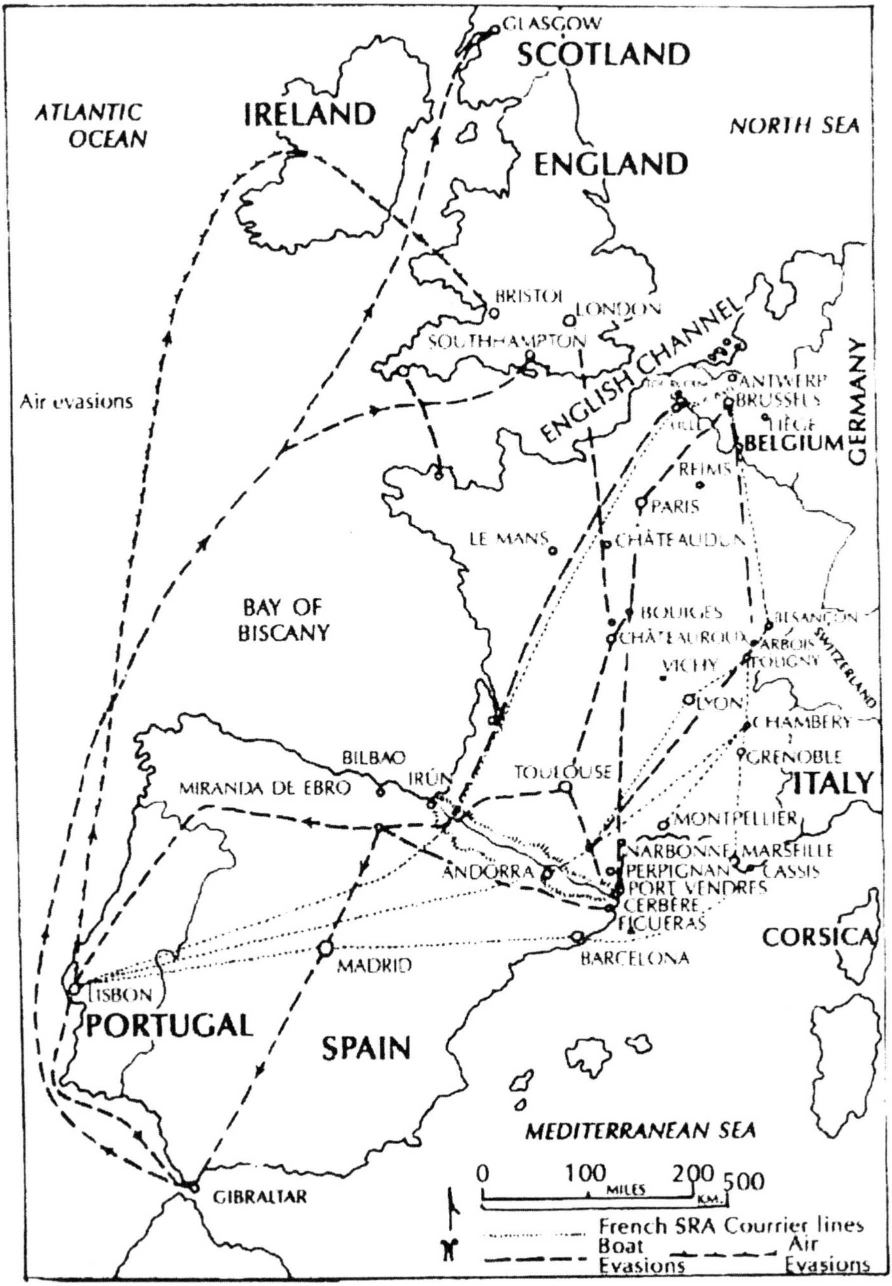

Main evasion routes and French courier lines (often changed)

Escape Line Map from June 2007 AFEES newsletter

Escape to England

At the beginning of January, 1942 Dad crossed the French border near La Chapelle on advice from cavalry captain Stanislaw Lomnicki. He was taken to a Foreigners' Labour Camp in Roanne where he was put to work in a coal mine from February to April. He was issued with a worker's identity card and gave his address as living at Montceaux les Mines. By June, 1942 he was working and staying at Saint Etienne, a small town south of Lyon. He was now a car mechanic and worked for Societe Anonyme des Houilleres de Saint-Etienne, a mining company operating locally. This area had one of the largest coal mines in France and employed many foreign workers but luckily, this time my father did not go down the mine but was a mechanic instead. Societe Anonyme is a French business structure like a British limited company or American corporation. However, he was still part of the Polish military having been recruited in Lyon until he was demobilised in January, 1942.

In France my father picked up the language quite well (he was already fluent in German) and he used to tell a story about staying in a brothel to avoid capture. This may well have happened. Lyon was the centre of the Resistance although membership of the 'Resistance' was hard to join and the focus tended to be on talk rather than action. There were no guns or explosives and help from London remained in effect, impossible and unavailable. Refugees had been descending on Lyon in their thousands so every hotel and guesthouse was full to bursting. Rooms in brothels and 'safe houses' such as convents were therefore routinely used.

According to my father`s personal report life in Vichy France wasn't too bad. Restaurants and cafes were still open. My father states that "bread was not rationed, although bread cannot be sold earlier than 18 hours after baking." The free market does not exist or is heavily reduced and there is an increasing shortage of tin. He states that while he was working in the iron foundry (one of the jobs when he was interned) he found out that casts were produced every second week. Crude steel was supplemented with large amounts of scrap metal and there were frightening shortages of coal and coke. Gasoline was increasingly becoming rationed although the majority of medical doctors drove gasoline powered cars. Other citizens used charcoal powered vehicles.

Cigarettes were rationed and sugar was unobtainable. Numerous trains had been deleted from the timetables and the most important routes were served by buses. New roads were being built with the labour provided by internees. Dwelling conditions were very good with the houses clean and tidy. This applied too to the living conditions for the internees.

When it came to work in the factories it was almost impossible for foreigners. Emigration of many people near St. Etienne and Beaulieu caused relations between emigres and war exiles to become strained and almost hostile. There were accusations of 'work divesting', a situation which was to be repeated in England for my father a few years later. Coal mining was the main industry in that region and my father states in relation to finding work that "the worst are people who have the so-called, "strong backs" i.e. have friends in high places and protegees"

At the Polish canteen in Beaulieu my father made friends with Captain Brzozsko (Brzozko) who was chief of the canteen and took care of Poles escaping from German captivity. Brozozko also arranged talks on national questions.

Two other friends and allies were Captain Kowalski who was a devout patriot and organised celebrations of Polish national anniversaries, and Father Knapik who was a great friend of Polish escapees from German captivity.

From time to time, my father sent back to Poland small photographs taken during his time as an internee and as a worker in the Saint Etienne area to his mother and sister Maryla and one photograph shows him in a smart trenchcoat a la Maigret with the collar turned up and smoking a cigarette. Quite smart for war time. Luckily he used to put the dates and places on the back of the photographs and this one reads 'Beaulieu 1942'.

My father held a Combattants Volontaires des Guerres card right up to 1946 when he was finally in England. This was an award, including a medal, that was given by the French for acts of resistance including internship and he must have been proud to have belonged to such an auspicious organisation.

Beaulieu, 1942

Not forgetting the specific orders by General Sikorski to get to England at all costs to help fight the war, my father was assisted by a Polish secret organisation and of course 'Brzozko', as well as senior sergeant Banach and warrant officer Kozien to leave France, crossing the French border near Marseille. He doesn't detail how he got to Marseille from the Saint Etienne area but he was helped by Polish officers with travel documents and liaison. These transfers from France to Britain were often organised by 'Brzozko' and were strictly secret and very dangerous. Among other men who helped his escape, particularly from Switzerland was the Swiss farmer whom he had worked for previously, Mr Hauser, verifying my mother's later account. In contrast, he states that the institution that made it more difficult was the Polish consulate in Bern. They didn't find anywhere for him to stay or give him food.

Another person who helped escaping Poles at that time was Captain Decker, a Roman catholic who converted from evangelism in France and was tragically killed by a bomb during a German air raid in June,

1942. In contrast, my father came across a person in May, 1942 whilst he was working in the labour camp in Roanne that he suspected to be a German officer pretending to be a Pole. His name was Ferdynand and he used documents issued for a person of Polish nationality. He insisted that my father should return to Poland as a Volksdeutsch and promised to cover his travelling expenses and help him to find a job there. A 'Volksdeutsch' was a person of Eastern European nationality whose language and culture were of German origins but who did not hold German citizenship. The Nazi term (possibly coined by Hitler) in the 1930s and 1940s carried overtones of blood and race that were difficult to explain by a simple English translation. 'Volksdeutsche', numbering about 30 million, lived outside the Reich, a significant number living in Poland, Ukraine, Romania, and the Baltic States. Some memoir literature attests to members of the Volksdeutsche contributing more than silent acquiescence to the betrayal and murder of their Jewish neighbours during the Holocaust. Little wonder my father was sceptical and suspicious of this man.

Flight from Marseille was again laborious and long. Leaving France on 14 June, 1942 he arrived in Gibraltar five days later. Using a well-known escape route some weeks later in July he finally arrived in Great Britain and landed in Glasgow. From there he was sent to Blackpool where he arrived on 30 July, 1942. It was more than a month after he had left France and his thoughts and feelings must have been in a mixture of turmoil and relief. He had a detailed 'debriefing' to complete which contained most of the facts that I have described and, I suspect, written in his own hand. On the very last page he details what he witnessed as normal, everyday life in Vichy France and the underlying propaganda on both sides.

> "In general, people are waiting for liberation by the English together with allied forces. Sometimes clear pro-German trends happen, caused by propaganda or present developments in war activities. German propaganda can be seen in books and newspapers that attack bolshevism." He adds, "In almost every factory there are some Germans who have access to all activities going on there (according to a report by Klein, a Frenchman in Roanne)."

He goes on:

> "English propaganda also exists in flyers dropped by the RAF, wall inscriptions in streets and in public conveniences. Local people treat this kind of propaganda positively but also wanted assurances and advice, as well as some explanation of present war attitudes in order to lift their spirits. They suffer from permanent fear, for instance 14 Frenchmen were recently arrested for reading English flyers."

Other 'Escape and Evasion reports' from Polish men during the war included the following:

> "I landed near Calais , but there was a very strong wind and my parachute opened late, so that I broke some bones in my foot. I hid my parachute and made inland. For the next 48 hours I moved only at night, and hid during the day, but owing to my damaged foot progress was very slow. On 10 Nov I spoke to a boy and told him who I was. He told me to wait, returning within an hour with his father and a wheelbarrow. I was taken to a farm behind a big house where I was kept for six days. The owner of the house gave me civilian clothes and money. While I was there a priest came to the house and brought a French identity card for me."

And another one:

> "I spent the night in a small hotel, where I was given a meal, although I had no food card. I had been living on fruit. Next morning I took the train to Besancon. There I was taken to a house. In the evening a man arrived with a lorry. He had been in the French Air Force in the last war. He took me to a small farm near the Line of Demarcation, where I spent two nights. On 25 Nov he drove me to the Line of Demarcation near a wood. I went on alone through this small wood of about two kilometres, and saw Chamblay on my right. I walked on to Vaudrey, some eight kilometres further. There I went to the Gendarmerie, where I said I was an escaper from a German camp. They gave me a bus ticket to Lons-le-Saunier, and a train ticket to Lyons, and told me to report to the Polish Demobilisation Camp."

What appears surprising is the amount of help and assistance many of the Polish escapees received from the French, both local people and the authorities. It seems there was help and a willingness to assist the Allies as the French looked forward to liberation.

Polish squadron, Dad second from right

Finally, he flies

From debriefing my Dad was sent to RAF Station Halton for six months to undergo training. Early in 1943 he obtained a IIndclass certificate as an airframe rigger and was posted in February 1943 to join 300 Bomber Squadron for technical duties.

300 (Masovian) Polish Bomber Squadron had been formed at RAF Bramcote, Warwickshire in 1940. It was one of several Polish squadrons in the Second World War and it was formed as part of an agreement between the Polish Government in Exile and the UK. Polish officers were in command with British advisers and the total number of Polish airmen in Polish squadrons at that time totalled between 400 and 500. A clause had been added to the Anglo-Polish agreement that the whole of the Polish Air Force would operate under Polish military law rather than King's Regulations. The airmen had to swear two oaths; one to their own Government and one to the King. Their uniforms were the same as the RAF (made by Austin Reed) but with 'Poland' on the shoulder. I know my father wore his uniform with great pride.

The seat of the Polish government in England at that time was at Stratton House, Piccadilly with the Polish Red Cross in Belgrave Square and the Embassy in Portland Place. After the agreement between the two Allies was put together the Polish Air Force expanded to four bomber squadrons, two fighter squadrons and one section of army support.

The four Polish squadrons were then transferred to Swinderby, Lincs and retrained on Wellington bombers. The squadrons used several versions of the Wellington bombers and in 1941 the unit was flying from Hemswell on 'gardening' (mining) operations. The squadron's Intelligence Officer was Michael Bentine (later to become well-known as an entertainer). The unit was then re-equipped with Avro Lancaster bombers and continued to use these until the end of the war.

The squadron took part in notable air offensives in Europe including attacks on Nazi Germany's naval ships and other naval facilities in Wilhelmshaven and its U boat facilities in St. Nazaire. The last bombers to fly from Swinderby base was in 1946. Lancasters were bombing Germany from Ingham and later from Faldingworth.

Dad, Second from right

300 squadron

Following commencement of his training in aircrew category of Flight Engineer, a year later in 1944, my father was transferred to the 301 Special Duties Squadron stationed in Brindisi, Italy. In 1944, 301 squadron had taken over the duties of 1586 squadron and was renamed in Brindisi itself. Their duties included flying supply missions to occupied Europe.

On my Dad's return he was moved in July 1944 to the 318 Fighter and Reconnaissance Squadron. He volunteered for aircrew duties and on 7 March, 1945 he completed his training as a Flight Engineer in July on Lancaster bombers and finally returned to 300 Squadron. Unfortunately there is no record of his particular duties in Italy but, most importantly, in September, 1945 he had met my mother who was a WAAF at the NAAFI club in Lincoln. She was from Sheffield and had been called up in 1943. She worked at the Signals Centre at Waddington and a few months later Mum and Dad were engaged and finally married in church in June, 1946 following a previous ceremony at a Registry Office in May.

300 squadron continued raiding ground targets throughout the spring of 1944. Lancasters were bombing Germany from the bases at Ingham and later Faldingworth. 300 crew were involved in the bombing of Dresden and also in the last major operation of the Polish Air Force – the great raid by 14 Lancasters on Berchtesgaden, Hitler's Eagles Nest retreat on 25 April, 1945. On 8 May, 1945 VE day Group Captain Robert Beill assembled the men and reminded them that 300 squadron had won 106 British gallantry awards and 15 commendations. He did not tell them that the squadron had suffered more deaths than any other bomber squadron in the RAF. The next day a message was received from the Air Council. They sent their greetings and congratulations to all ranks of the Polish Air Force stating that `they do not forget that you were the first to resist the aggressor, neither do they forget that you came after manifold trials to our aid and when we most needed your help`.

Following offensive missions, 300 squadron took part in Operation Manna – the dropping of food supplies to the Dutch; 'Exodus', the repatriation of British ex-POWs to Great Britain; 'Dodge', the transport of British troops from Italy to Britain; and the carrying of Red Cross supplies for liberated Poles in German concentration camps.

My father was now Flight Sergeant Navigator and from his log book he flew many hours from Faldingworth in 1946. He was involved in practice air to sea landings, 'wastage' flights, formation flights and bombing circle landings. He was too late to see combative action but clocked up the flying time he had been wanting to do since he was a young cadet in Poland.

In October 1946 my Dad was given a reference from his Polish Squadron Leader, B Jarkowski and it read: 'An efficient and conscientious Flight Engineer who has shown much professional ability and eagerness for flying.'

The previous March the Government had announced that the Polish Squadrons were to be disbanded after the Allies had withdrawn their support for the Polish Government and my father had to leave his beloved Lancasters. He was awarded The Medal Lotniczy and one Bar and British commemorative decorations. Foreign decorations included the 1939/1945 Star, and the Italy Star.

Brindisi 1944, Dad on left

Dad

Lancaster, Dunholme 1945

Building a new life

The Poles had a history of deportation by Stalin since 1940. After Russia invaded Poland 1.7 million Poles were deported to slave labour camps in Siberia, Kazakhstan and the north. It was a terrible ordeal with journeys lasting weeks. There was little food or shelter and the journey culminated in work in the mines, on farms or remote logging camps. There was no medical attention and food was barely enough to survive on and yet the work was incredibly hard. Only a third of this forced deportation survived. This is one of the accounts of the Poles in WW2 that is rarely told, but in England the air crews of 300 Bomber Squadron coming towards the end of the war were only too aware of their fate in Russia if England did not take them in.

In March, 1946 the Government announced that the Polish forces were to be disbanded. Clement Attlee (Prime Minister at the time) felt little sympathy for the Poles and the Labour Government as a whole saw Poles as Fascists. 30% of the Government favoured allowing Poles to remain: 56% for deportation. On 6 June, 1946 there was a Victory Parade held in London. Poles were excluded from these celebrations.

Shortly before, on 20 May Ernest Bevin had formed the Polish Resettlement Corps. Nearly 3,000 Poles opted to return to Poland and a very uncertain future. 11,000 joined the Resettlement Corps giving them the right to remain. The Polish Resettlement Corps 1947 was finally put into law and was the first mass immigration legislation of the United Kingdom. It offered British citizenship to over 250,000 displaced Polish troops on British soil who had fought against Nazi Germany and opposed the Soviet takeover of Poland.

Under the Resettlement Corps Poles could enlist for a period of demobilisation. Temporary accommodation was found in former army and air force camps and military hospitals. The Resettlement Corps was disbanded after demobbing all the soldiers and airmen in 1949. And so my father signed up for two years for Regular Air Force service. This was in January, 1947. He was already married and my mother was expecting me in May 1947. They did not find accommodation in one of the camps but shared a small cottage with an elderly lady and paid half rent. After I was born (they were at my mother's home in Sheffield for the birth) they returned to Lincoln and stayed with friends.

In 1948 Dad was serving in Framlingham, Suffolk and in January he reported that he was suffering from severe psoriasis. This skin disease was to stay with him the whole of his life and perhaps it had been brought on through all the difficulties he had experienced during the War. Nevertheless he was not due a pension and neither were any of the Polish soldiers or airmen.

In March, 1946 the Government had announced that the Polish forces were to be disbanded including the Polish squadrons. Squadron 300 was disbanded in October. It had been the longest in action and suffered the highest losses. It had been well known amongst the Polish forces that return to Poland may almost certainly have meant forced imprisonment by Stalin in the very north of Russia with little hope of survival or reprieve. It was important and necessary for my father that he remain in England with his family and make a new life in this country. Clement Attlee, Prime Minister of the Labour Government at that time felt little sympathy for the Poles and the Labour Government saw the Poles as fascists. The Poles were afraid to go back as they may have been seen as enemies of the new Communist regime and imprisoned or shot. But there was a greater danger.

The Yalta Conference in February 1945 had been a deciding factor on the fate of the Poles in England and elsewhere. This was the post WW2 conference held at Crimea and was a meeting of the three heads of government: the United States, the United Kingdom and the Soviet Union discussed the post-war reorganisation of Germany and Europe. There have been many criticisms of the procedure of this conference and its outcomes. Roosevelt was seriously ill at the time and appeared unable to fully take part; Churchill has also been criticised for his seemingly passive acceptance of the Soviet domination of Poland and Eastern Europe. Stalin had made a genuine concession in finally agreeing to a French zone in Germany, while Churchill and Roosevelt had given in a great deal on Poland. The conclusion was that Eastern Europe had been conceded de facto to Josef Stalin by Franklin D. Roosevelt and Winston Churchill as early as the Tehran Conference in November 1943, and finally at Yalta.

There was no question at all that my father would return to his homeland. It had changed beyond all recognition. Warsaw had fallen at the beginning of the war and little was left of it. My father's main concern was internment again possibly in the far north of Russia in the Gulag, a system of prisons which had imprisoned millions of people.

And so my parents decided to stay in England and try to make their lives in this country. It wasn't easy, there were overt expressions of hostility. There were confrontations and fights. Placards read "Poles go home" and "England for the English". Still wearing their uniforms, the Polish airmen were jeered in the streets, so much so that many removed the `Poland` flashes on their sleeves to blend in more easily. They produced their own Polish newspapers to liaise and keep in touch. When it came to getting jobs, the Unions were difficult. The TUC kept them out so the mining industry was effectively closed to them. The National Union of Agricultural Workers also kept them out. The Government's policy at that time was that the Poles could help rebuild the country. The Press were divided: The 'Sunday Times' and 'The Daily Telegraph' defended the Poles; 'The Times', the 'Daily Mirror', the News Chronicle', The Star' and the 'Evening 'Standard' all fanned many groundless fears of unemployment for British nationals together with unfounded claims of black marketeering.

In January 1947 there was a softening and the NUM union finally agreed to admit Poles and by the summer 2,000 Poles were working down the mines.

Some Poles could not, and never would get over the war. They were demoralised and they could only do enough to be able to bring home enough money for their families. Brave and nationalistic, their courage was indomitable. Their new lives were beginning but just surviving meant those times must have seemed insurmountable.

My father had been demobbed twice, once from the Polish Army in Lyon, France in January, 1942 and again from the Polish section of the RAF in January, 1949. His brief Statement of Discharge was in the form of a Certificate which could be used as a testament to good behaviour and trade proficiency and therefore extremely useful for looking for a job in the civilian arena. The Polish Air Force also detailed his previous education, his rank and the medals he had won. His birth certificate was a different matter. It was unobtainable and my father had been told that the Germans had destroyed all the records. However, in 1963 (when we

Mum and Dad

first visited our relatives in Poland) copies were made of his certificate which probably made looking for work a little easier.

Following two years in the Polish Resettlement Corps my parents decided to move to London, probably because there was a greater chance of work in the capital. My father`s upbringing was invaluable. He took classes at the Licensed College and attained a Licensed Trade Diploma for Staff Training. Mum was living with friends in Lincoln as Dad tried to get work in London. Eventually he worked at the Dorchester Hotel putting his Silver Service skills to good use. They lived at a retired Dr`s house in Royal Crescent, Lancaster Gate, opposite Hyde Park. A good address now but at that time shortly after the war it no doubt was grim. My mother did some work for the Dr whilst living there and helped prepare meals; my father probably did some work too.

Undeterred by their wish to remain and work in England together with all the other immigrants who helped to win the war, my parents heard that the Government was offering nationalisation under the British Nationality Act 1948 creating the new status of citizen of the United Kingdom. This gave further protection to my father from being sent back to Poland and ultimately the danger of transportation to Russia. To try to achieve some anonymity and to blend with British born people, he changed our surname. My mother and father became Kayworth, not Kaminski and my name changed from Kaminska to Kayworth. Non-acceptance and outward hostility were difficult barriers for my father and as work was scarce resentment towards the Poles always simmered below the surface.

The Certificate of Naturalisation and change of name was completed in May, 1950 and when my brother was born the following year, his surname was Kayworth. My father`s old and new names were published in The London Gazette, 16 June 1950 together with a full page of immigrants also wishing for naturalisation from Poland, Denmark, Russia, USA, Palestine, Norway, Greece, Rumania, Czechoslovakia, Hungary. Many of these people were listed as Polish with occupations as diverse as miner, poultry farmer, writer, bottle sorter, engineer, bank clerk, some still serving in the Forces. All of them wanted a better life in Britain with new futures for their families, at the same time helping to rebuild a battered country with their skills, imagination and indomitable natures.

Life continued to be hard. My parents moved away from London towards Southall and the suburbs. He was still a member of the RAF and most years collected for them on Armistice Day. He also joined the British Legion and served as a representative of the RAF on the Service Committee. Always striving to learn and improve the family finances, my father did some college courses part time but up to this time my parents had been renting accommodation and had been evicted once. They wanted to buy their own house, as so many did, and my father approached the RAF Association, the British Legion and members of my mother`s family to put some money together for a deposit. They finally managed to do this but my father`s health had deteriorated after a heart attack in the 1960s. After a few years in Nottingham they retired to Scarborough. My father had a few jobs but his health was not good and in 1973 he had his third stroke which left him with a speech impediment and slight paralysis. He managed to read widely and also gave private German lessons locally. He never forgot Poland and his upbringing.

My Aunt Maryla and her son Andrzez came to stay with us in the summer of 1960. It was the first time we had met any of our Polish relatives although we had known a few of our father`s Polish friends over the years. It had been difficult for them to leave Russian dominated Poland and I recall they said that it was important by the authorities that they go back to Poland after their visit. In 1963, after I left school my father took us on the long journey to Poland and after the sea crossing from the East coast and landing at Rotterdam we drove all the way to Szczecin in Northern Poland to stay with my grandmother and aunt. It was the first time we had met our grandmother. I recall the long journey and the check points we had to go through when my father told us to be quiet and pretend we were asleep. Entering Poland the tall, wooden lookout posts looked forbidding and frightening particularly in the dark and we had in the 1960s, entered a strange, poor and ravaged new world.

Coming back home we were still brought up to be English. We were taken out on Sundays as my father always had a car, visiting grand country homes, the National Trust and wooded areas. My father though always remained Polish and he visited Poland several more times: his heart belonged there.

In October, 1974 he died in Scarborough after a massive stroke and his ashes were spread in the local woodland he loved.

After he died, looking through his possessions we found that he had been working on a coat of arms. It had a rough drawn outline with a central shield and the words `Forti Nihil Difficile` which translates to: `Nothing is difficult for the Brave`, a fitting tribute to a man who overcame huge obstacles, both as a young man and throughout his life.

The last words of this account of a life lived must go to my father in a letter written to my brother:

> "All I can say about the SECOND WORLD WAR is that I myself, my friends and their friends were all reputed to be brave soldiers but that they never gave a thought to bravery and heroism any more than I did. It never occurred to us. We did our duty and that was that. When a dangerous mission came up and some of your comrades were married men with children, you just said to yourself: You're not married, so that took it for granted that was the whole style of our upbringing."

References

Swiss Federal Archives E5330-01#1975/95#13486 ref.98/1941/6554
Ibid

Polish (Sikorski) Institute ref. LOT-AVV96/21/24
Ibid

Ibid
`Bloody Foreigners` Robert Winder p.323

England, 1945

Southall, 1954

Southall, 1950s